HoLiDAY ORiGAMi

HOLIDAY ORIGAMI

By Jill Smolinski and Andrea Urton

Illustrations by Dianne O'Quinn Burke
and Mary Ann Fraser

Photographs by Ann Bogart

LOWELL HOUSE JUVENILE

LOS ANGELES

NTC/Contemporary Publishing Group

Published by Lowell House
A division of NTC/Contemporary Publishing Group, Inc.
4255 West Touhy Avenue, Lincolnwood (Chicago), Illinois 60646-1975 U.S.A.

Requests for such permissions should be addressed to:
NTC/Contemporary Publishing Group, Inc.
4255 West Touhy Avenue, Lincolnwood (Chicago), Illinois 60646-1975 U.S.A.

Managing Director and Publisher: Jack Artenstein
Director of Publishing Services: Rena Copperman
Editorial Director, Juvenile: Brenda Pope-Ostrow
Director of Juvenile Development: Amy Downing
Crafts Artist: Charlene Olexiewicz
Interior Design: Michele Lanci-Altomare
Cover Design: Lisa Raphael

Library of Congress Catalog Card Number: 98-67920
ISBN 0-7373-0094-9

Lowell House books can be purchased at special discounts
when ordered in bulk for premiums and special sales.
Contact Customer Service at the above address,
or call 1-800-323-4900.

Printed and bound in Hong Kong

10 9 8 7 6 5 4 3 2 1

CONTENTS

BEFORE YOU START

Every holiday calls for a special celebration, and now you can add spark to the occasion when you turn ordinary paper into origami art. All it takes is a piece of paper, a little patience, and lots of creativity. So get folding, and get ready for a whole year full of great holiday fun!

WHAT YOU'LL NEED

For folding your forms, any thin, square paper will do. You can buy origami craft paper that is colored on one side and white on the other at art supply and specialty stores. It's also precut into squares, with a standard size being about 6 inches. You may want to cut your own squares from gift wrapping paper, thin wallpaper samples, colored photocopying paper, notebook paper, or even paper bags! (Construction paper works well for big designs, but for most projects it's too thick to make the nice, sharp folds that you need.)

For each project, you'll find suggestions for materials and tips on decorating your origami crafts, but feel free to jazz them up any way you like.

BASIC FOLDS

There are three basic folds you will use throughout this book:

VALLEY FOLD

Fold the paper toward you.

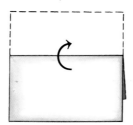

MOUNTAIN FOLD

Fold the paper away from you.

SQUASH FOLD

This fold is usually called for when two sides of a flap need to be squashed flat. To accomplish this, poke your finger inside the flap and—you guessed it—squash it.

BASIC FORMS

Many origami crafts begin with one of many basic forms. Here, you'll learn the forms that are the foundation for some of the origami projects in this book.

BASIC FORM 1

1 Begin with a square piece of paper in a flat diamond shape, color side face down. Fold your paper in half, bringing the left point to meet the right point. Then unfold to make a crease.

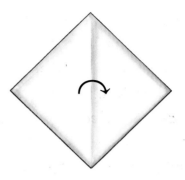

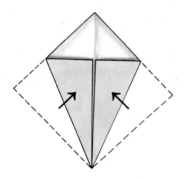

2 Fold the left and right sides to the center crease, so your paper looks like a kite.

BASIC FORM 2

1 Begin with a piece of paper in a flat square shape, color side face down. Fold the paper in half by bringing the top edge to meet the bottom edge, then fold it in half again by folding the left side to meet the right side. Reopen it into a square.

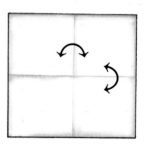

2 Next, fold each of the four corners to the center point, where the two creases made in Step 1 cross.

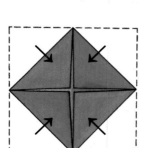

BASIC FORM 3

1 To make this form, begin with a square, color side face down. Fold your paper in half, side to side, then fold the top edge down to align with the bottom. Now open it up to the original square and fold it diagonally both ways. Reopen it.

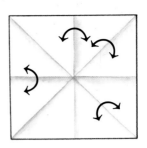

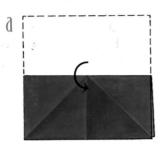

a

b

2 Fold the paper in half to make a rectangle. Then fold it in half again to make a small square. Lay the square flat on your table with the open ends facing down and to the right.

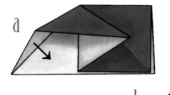

a

b

3 Now hold the top flap up straight and poke your finger inside until it reaches the very tip. Carefully squash the flap down to form a triangle. You should still be able to see part of the square from the other side. Be sure all your corners line up and look pointed. Now turn the form over and repeat this step on the other side.

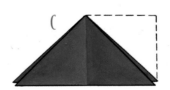

c

THE SECRET TO SUCCESS

In the art of origami, neatness counts. Always work on a smooth, hard surface, and make each crease as straight and crisp as possible. If you make a mistake, just chalk it up to experience and start over with a new piece of paper.

8

BASIC FORM 4

1 To make this form, you must first follow Step 1 in Basic Form 3, then unfold.

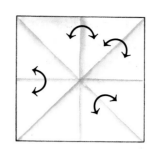

2 Lay out the origami square in front of you, in a diamond shape, color side face down. Fold the paper in half, bringing the top point to meet the bottom point.

3 Carefully hold the right side of the form open at Point C, then squash-fold it by pushing down on it to meet Point D. Does it look like illustration B here?

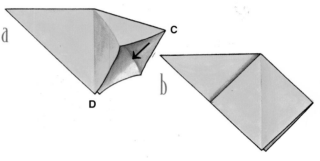

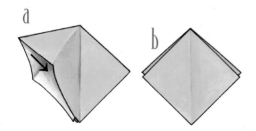

4 Repeat Step 3 with the left side of the form.

BASIC FORM 5

1 Begin with a piece of origami paper in a flat diamond shape, color side face down. Fold your paper in half, bringing the top point to meet the bottom.

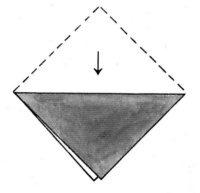

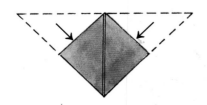

2 Now fold the far left and right points down to the center so that the points meet at the bottom of your form.

NiFTY NEW YEAR'S CONFETTI CONTAINER

For starters, why not kick off the New Year with a midnight surprise? Your friends will love these unforgettable party favors!

WHAT YOU'LL NEED

- one sheet of origami paper
- glitter glue • stencils
- markers • hole punch
- an assortment of colored paper

DIRECTIONS

1 Begin with Basic Form 4. With the open end of the origami paper facing up *away from you*, fold the left and right points (front flaps only) to the center.

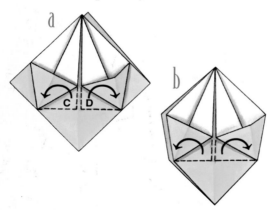

2 Now fold the left point out to the edge of the origami sheet, crease, and unfold. Repeat on the right side. Lift the left "arm" of the triangle, open it slightly, and press down on Point C to flatten it, then repeat this step with Point D.

3 Turn the form over, and repeat Steps 1 and 2 on the other side.

4 Grasp just the outer half of the left front flap and use a Mountain Fold to fold it back into the center. Repeat this step with the right front flap, then turn the form over and repeat this step on the other side.

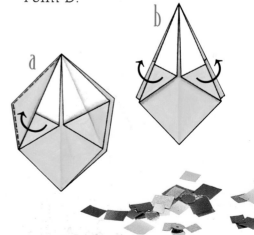

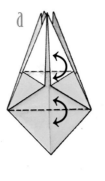

a

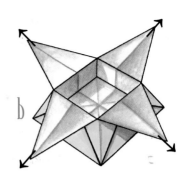

b

5 Fold the top point of your origami craft one-third of the way down, then fold the bottom portion one-third of the way up. Crease and unfold. Get ready to transform this craft into a star-shaped box. First, gently tug the front and back points apart from each other. Then use your fingers to press the box into shape, flattening the base to the first crease and folding back all the sides at the second crease.

6 Add some sparkle by rolling glitter glue on the form. Use stencils to outline one digit of the New Year on each flap, such as 1-9-9-9. As you color in each stenciled number, balance the flap on a hard surface.

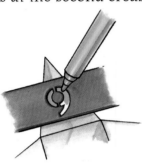

7 With the hole punch, punch out lots of small circles from the colored paper to use as confetti. Fill your party favors with confetti, then close each box by fold-ing its flaps over to cover the contents

HATFUL OF FUN

To ring in the New Year, create festive paper hats for your friends and family! By using paper of different sizes, you can make a hat to fit anyone.

WHAT YOU'LL NEED

- origami or wrapping paper
- wire cutters • wire garland (available at craft or party stores)
- stapler • assorted colors of curling ribbon
- hole punch • large marker or paintbrush with a round handle
- elastic cord

DIRECTIONS

1. For a hat to fit your head, you'll need a piece of paper minimum size 18 inches by 18 inches. Begin with Basic Form 5, with the two loose points facing you. Fold up the front flaps only of the two bottom points to the top point. Then fold these two points out to the sides as shown.

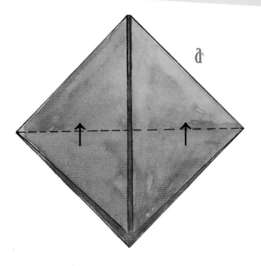

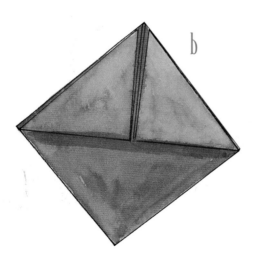

2 Take the new front bottom flap and fold up three-quarters of it toward the top of the hat. Then take the bottom edge of this flap and fold it up to the halfway point.

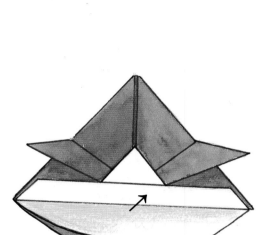

3 Tuck in the back flap, and your hat is ready to be decorated.

4 With wire cutters, cut a length of wire garland for the rim of the hat. Secure garland onto the hat with three or four staples.

5 Cut 24-inch lengths of assorted color curling ribbon. With the hole punch, punch a hole through the hat, approximately half an inch down from the top point.

6 Neatly gather the curling ribbon ends together and thread them through the hole. When the ribbons are pulled halfway through, secure them to the hat by tying the ribbons in a knot. Have an adult help you use scissors to curl the ribbons.

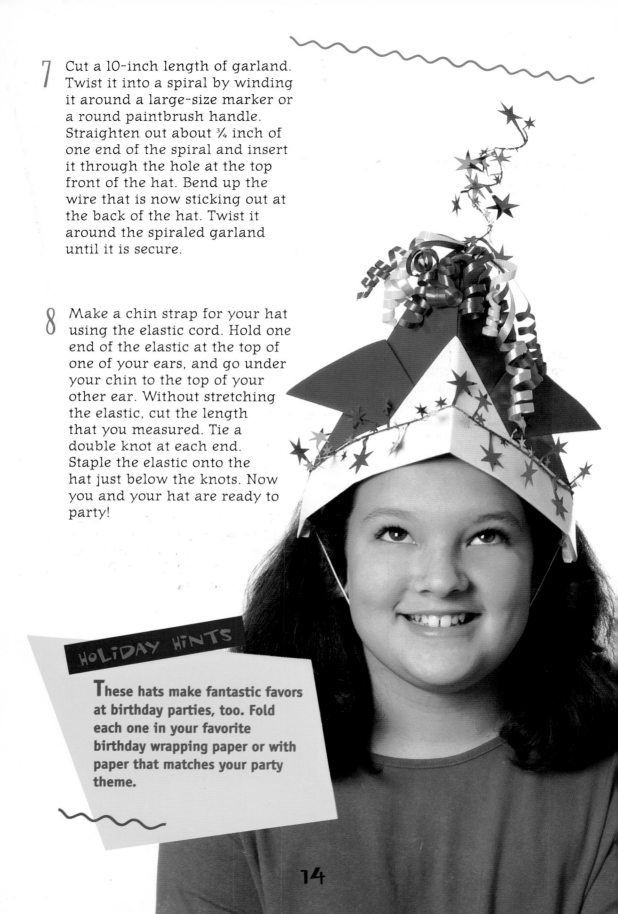

7 Cut a 10-inch length of garland. Twist it into a spiral by winding it around a large-size marker or a round paintbrush handle. Straighten out about ¾ inch of one end of the spiral and insert it through the hole at the top front of the hat. Bend up the wire that is now sticking out at the back of the hat. Twist it around the spiraled garland until it is secure.

8 Make a chin strap for your hat using the elastic cord. Hold one end of the elastic at the top of one of your ears, and go under your chin to the top of your other ear. Without stretching the elastic, cut the length that you measured. Tie a double knot at each end. Staple the elastic onto the hat just below the knots. Now you and your hat are ready to party!

HOLIDAY HINTS

These hats make fantastic favors at birthday parties, too. Fold each one in your favorite birthday wrapping paper or with paper that matches your party theme.

14

FLUTTERING BUTTERFLY

This springtime butterfly is easy to make and is the perfect adornment for a friend's valentine card or gift.

WHAT YOU'LL NEED
- origami paper • pipe cleaners
- wire cutters • glue • scissors

DIRECTIONS

1 Begin with your paper folded in half like the first step in Basic Form 3, then unfold it so it is lying flat in a square shape. Fold the right and left sides so they meet the center line.

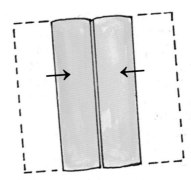

2 Now fold the bottom and top edges so they meet the center line. Then make a nice sharp crease and unfold the top and bottom edges only.

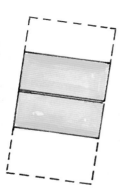

3 Your form should now look like this. Make two diagonal creases across the center four squares only. Do this first by folding point A to meet point B. Crease the paper sharply, then unfold it. Now repeat this step on the opposite side, bringing point C to meet point D.

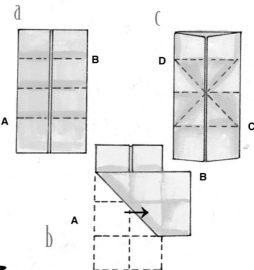

4 This next step is tricky, so look closely at the illustration for help. First, grasp the bottom two corners. Then lift them up and gently tug them apart so they flatten and the bottom edge meets the center. Repeat this step with the top two corners, only this time pull them down to meet the center.

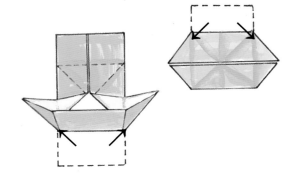

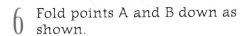

5 Use a Mountain Fold to fold the form in half, open side up.

6 Fold points A and B down as shown.

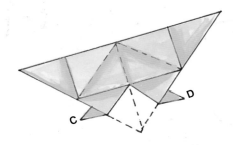

7 Turn the form over, then fold it in half and unfold it to make a sharp crease between the butterfly's wings. Turn out points C and D to give the back of each smaller wing more shape.

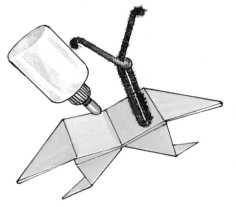

8 For the body, bend a pipe cleaner in half. Twist it once around at the spot that is to be the head. Spread out the two pipe cleaner ends to create antennae. Cut any excess with the wire cutters. Glue the body onto the wings.

9 Add beautiful designs to your butterfly by cutting out a variety of colorful shapes from origami paper. Shapes can include circles, diamonds, triangles, teardrops, stripes, and so on. Glue the shapes onto the wings of the butterfly.

HOLIDAY HINTS

Many people give flowers to loved ones on Valentine's Day, but how about springing a bouquet of butterflies on a few favorite friends? Just attach each butterfly to the end of a long green pipe cleaner or wire wrapped in green tape. Stick the bunch in a vase—it's a fun treat that will last all year long!

SECRET POCKET VALENTINE

Every February 14th, you have an extra-special reason to send a friend a note saying you care. This Valentine's Day, send a secret message to your favorite Valentine in a heart-shaped card that's tucked in an elegant origami envelope.

WHAT YOU'LL NEED

- one sheet each of red origami paper, pink origami paper, and white origami paper
- two stickers • clear tape
- marker • scissors • paper doilies
- glue • pearl beads
- ribbon • hole punch

DIRECTIONS

1. To make the heart-shaped card, you'll first need to complete Steps 1 through 6 of the Lucky Four-Leaf Clover (page 20), using red paper.

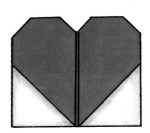

2. Then tuck under the left and right edges behind the heart to finish your one-of-a-kind Valentine. Set it aside.

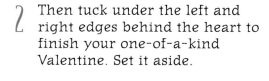

3. With another square of paper the same size that you used for your card, you'll now make an envelope. Using pink paper, begin with Basic Form 2.

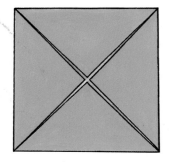

4 Unfold the top point, then seal where the other three points meet with one of the stickers. (If you don't have a sticker, a small piece of clear tape will work fine.)

5 Now fold the top point back down so it overlaps the center by about ½ inch. Set it aside.

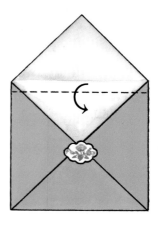

6 Take another small square of paper and write your Valentine's message on it. Fold it and slip your note between the folds on the front of the origami heart, like a pocket.

7 With scissors, cut paper doilies to fit inside your heart card and the envelope. Glue a cut-out doily to the front of the heart, leaving at least ¼-inch solid red border. Next, take your envelope and glue a doily onto the back side, leaving at least ½-inch solid colored border. Take the pearl beads and ribbon and decorate further as you wish. Set the crafts aside until the glue is dry.

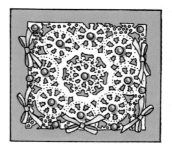

8 Then, with your hole punch, punch a hole in the corner of your envelope, about ½ inch beneath the top. Thread a ribbon through the hole, tying it in a big bow. Stick your card in the envelope, then seal it with the second sticker . . . and a kiss!

HOLIDAY HINTS

Spritz your Valentine card first with your favorite cologne (just a small squirt will do!) before handing it over for special delivery.

LUCKY FOUR-LEAF CLOVER

WHAT YOU'LL NEED

- four sheets of green origami paper
- glue • pipe cleaners
- green sequins • green glitter

Share a little luck o' the Irish with your friends by passing out these Lucky Four-Leaf Clovers on St. Patrick's Day.

DIRECTIONS

1. The clover is a four-part form. To make one leaf, begin with your paper in a flat square shape, colored side face down. Fold the paper in half, then in half the other way, creasing it firmly. Unfold the entire form.

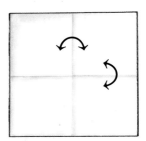

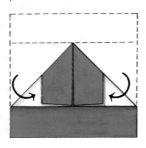

2. Now fold the top edge to the center crease, turn your form over, and fold the top left and right edges to meet in the center.

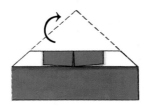

3. Using a Mountain Fold, fold the topmost point back so that the tip just meets the bottom of the origami sheet.

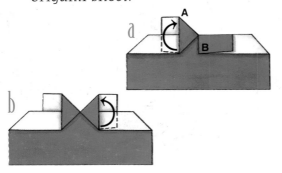

4. Ready to do a squash fold? Lift Point A, then poke your finger in and squash it flat so it looks like the illustration shown here. Repeat this step on Point B.

5 Fold the left and right sides to the center line, then fold in the two top left and right corners. Turn the form over.

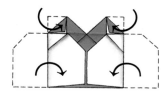

6 Just use a Mountain Fold to fold back the two topmost peaks $\frac{1}{4}$ inch or so, and your first heart-shaped leaf is complete.

7 Make three more clover shapes, repeating Steps 1 through 6 to do so. Join the pieces of your clover by putting some glue on the flap of Point H, then tucking it into the form along with Point G, repeating this step so the points of each leaf meet in the center.

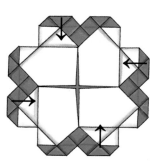

8 To create a clover stem, glue a green pipe cleaner to the back of the clover. To make your clover sparkle, glue on some green sequins or sprinkle some green glitter in the center or along the leaves. As long as you have the Lucky Four-Leaf Clover, no one will dare pinch you on St. Patty's Day!

HOLIDAY HINTS

To make a St. Patrick's Day pin, simply tape a safety pin to the back of your clover. Be sure to tape the side that does *not* open and close the pin. Wear it all day to send good-luck greetings to everyone you meet.

BRiNG ON THE BUNNY

Create a little Easter rabbit that is so cute, you'll want to leave it out all year long!

WHAT YOU'LL NEED

- two sheets of white origami paper
- clear tape • glue • cotton ball
- googly eye decorations • pink pom-pom
- two toothpicks • markers

DiRECTiONS

1. This is a two-part form. You'll start by making the bunny's body. To do this, begin with Basic Form 1, putting the smaller point toward you. Fold the top point down to where the left and right sides of the form meet, then fold it back again halfway up.

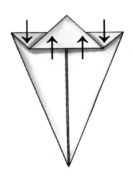

2. Fold the entire sheet in half lengthwise, using a Valley Fold. Now, at the thin end of the kite shape, carefully make a cut one-third the length of your form.

3. Lay the origami flat, with the smallest end on the left. To make big bunny ears, fold just the front left flap back to align with the bunny's body. That's the first ear. Make another ear by repeating this step on the back flap, only this time using a Mountain Fold.

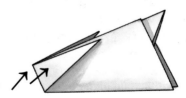

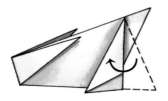

4. Now take the front flap on the right and fold it forward, keeping the bottom edges aligned. Turn the bunny over and repeat to complete its set of hind legs. Your bunny's body is finished.

5 To make its head, begin with a square piece of paper exactly half the size that you used to make the body, folding it so you have Basic Form 1.

a

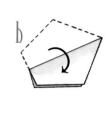
b

6 Take the bottommost point and fold it up to the top point where the two sides meet. Fold the form in half so that the point you just folded up is inside the fold.

7 Now you're ready to slip the head piece inside the body, lining up the two forms along their bottom edges. Tape the head in place.

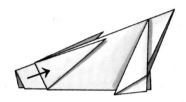

8 Give your rabbit some cute Easter bunny features. Glue a cotton ball to its end for a tail, add silly eyes that you buy at a craft store (or draw them in yourself), and add a pink pom-pom for its nose. For whiskers, ask a parent to poke two tiny holes in each side of the bunny's nose. Thread a toothpick through the bottom hole on the right side of its nose to the top hole on its left side. The second toothpick should be threaded through the top hole on the right side to the hole on the bottom left. The toothpicks should cross in the center. With markers or colored pencils, draw pink triangles inside the ears and lightly sketch in hind legs as shown.

HOLiDAY HiNTS

If you make your bunny using an 8-inch square of paper for its body, it will be just the right size to hide a decorated egg underneath. Who says bunnies can't lay eggs?

EGG-o-RAMA!

Decorating eggs has never been so much fun or so easy! With colorful origami paper and brightly colored markers or paints, these eggs will be the best in the basket—and they're unbreakable!

WHAT YOU'LL NEED

- two sheets of origami paper, same color
- glue • markers • puff paints
- paper cut-outs • glitter • stickers
- ribbon • a small treat

DIRECTIONS

1 Begin with one piece of paper flat in a diamond shape, then fold the paper in half by bringing the bottom to meet the top, so it forms a triangle.

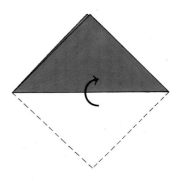

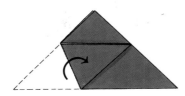

2 Take hold of the left lower point, and fold it across the form to touch the edge of the right side, keeping its top edge straight horizontally. Repeat this step using the lower right point, folding it so it meets the left side.

3 Give the bottom of your form rounded corners by using a Valley Fold to fold Points A and B, creasing them sharply, then unfolding. Now use an Inside-Reverse Fold to hide those points inside the form. To do this, start with Point A first, slightly lifting the flap and opening it up, then use your finger to poke in the point so it rests inside the form. Repeat this step with Point B.

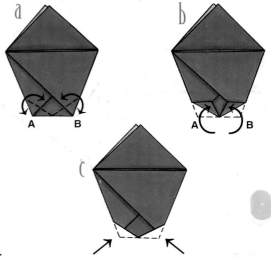

4 All that's left to do is tuck the front upper flap into the front triangle and the back upper flap into the remaining opening. That's one-half of your egg!

5 To make the other half, repeat Steps 1 through 4 with another sheet of paper.

6 It's simple to piece your egg together. Just unfold the back flap of one of the forms. Rub some glue on it, then slide it into the back pocket of the other form. Make sure that the plain sides of each egg half face toward the front. (You'll just see a horizontal crease line through the middle.)

7 Decorate your Easter egg with markers, paints, paper cut-outs, glitter, or stickers.

8 Glue a ribbon along the center crease, letting about 6 inches hang loose on either side. Let it dry, then if you want to, sneak a treat into your egg, such as jelly beans or a small toy. Seal the egg halves shut in back with a sticker, then tie the ribbon to look like a sash.

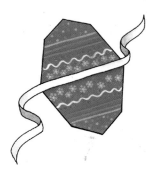

HOLIDAY HINTS

Create an Easter tree! It's easy—just make at least a dozen Egg-o-rama Easter eggs. Attach a looped piece of string to the top of each egg with tape or glue, then hang them all over a miniature tree or large plant.

PATRIOTIC PINWHEELS

Who needs fireworks on the Fourth of July? With simple origami steps, create a Patriotic Pinwheel in red, white, and blue that really works!

WHAT YOU'LL NEED

- **one sheet each of blue origami paper and red origami paper**
- **white stick-on stars or white puff paint**
- **glue • two Popsicle® sticks**
- **thumbtack**
- **small piece of cork**
- **colored ribbon • clear tape**

DIRECTIONS

1 Begin with a piece of blue paper in a square, folded so you have Basic Form 2, then unfold it so your paper is lying flat in a square, color side down. Fold the right and left sides to meet at the center line.

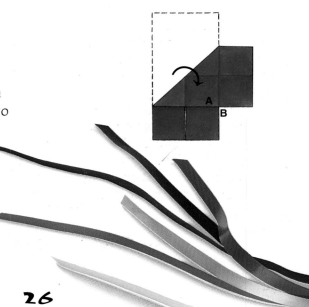

2 Now fold the bottom and top edges so they meet at the horizontal center line. Make a sharp crease, then unfold it.

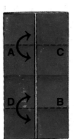

3 Make two diagonal creases across the center four squares only. To do this, fold Point A to meet Point B. Crease the paper sharply, then unfold it. Repeat this step on the opposite side, bringing Point C to meet Point D.

4 This next step is tricky, so look closely at the illustration for help. First, grasp the two bottom corners. Then lift them up and gently tug them apart so they flatten, and the bottom edge meets the center. Repeat this step with the two top corners, only this time pull them down to meet the center.

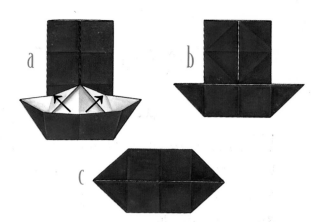

a

b

c

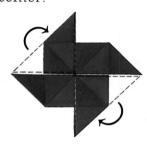

5 Look at the points on the left and right sides of your form. To make a pinwheel, just take the top half of the left point and lift it up so it points straight up. Then take the bottom half of the right point and pull it so it points straight down.

6 Now get your red paper, which should be about half the size you used to make your first pinwheel. Make another wheel by repeating Steps 1 through 5.

7 Add stars to the blue pinwheel using stick-ons or white puff paints. Glue two Popsicle® sticks together to make a long handle.

8 Lay the red form inside the middle of the blue one. Secure them both to the handle by sticking a thumbtack through the tiny hole in their centers, through the Popsicle® stick, and finally, into the small piece of cork. The tack should be covered in the cork to keep you from getting poked. The tack shouldn't go through the paper or your pinwheel won't whirl. Wrap a piece of ribbon around the stick, taping it at the top and the bottom of the handle. Now just pucker up and blow!

HoLiDAY HiNTS

Make streamers for the end of your pinwheel by cutting long, thin strips of red, white, and blue ribbon. Glue them to the bottom of the stick.

SMiLiN' JACK

The scariest day of the year for many kids is October 31—Halloween. You can create a jack-o'-lantern that's as cute and friendly as can be or more frightening than your worst nightmare (almost).

WHAT YOU'LL NEED

- orange origami paper
- black marker • green pipe cleaner

DIRECTIONS

1 Using the orange paper, begin with Basic Form 3. Fold the left and right front flaps up to the top center point, then turn the form over and repeat.

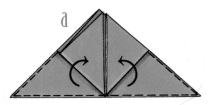

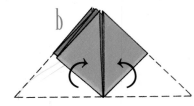

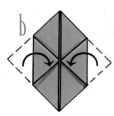

2 You should now have a small diamond shape in front of you. Fold the front left and right points to the center line. Turn the form over again and repeat this step on the other side.

3 Set your origami in front of you lengthwise, putting the side with the loose flaps at the top. Take the two front flaps only and tuck them into the center triangles. To do this, open the triangle pockets with your fingers and slip the edge in. Then turn your form over and repeat this step on the other side.

4 Pick up the right flap and close it as though you were turning the page of a book. The plain side of the form should now be showing. Turn the form over and repeat.

5 Use the black marker to draw a scary face on your pumpkin. On the other side, draw a happy or funny face.

6 Find the tiny hole at the bottom of your form. When you blow into it, your pumpkin will puff up right before your eyes. Push on the squared edges gently with your finger to "round" out the form a bit.

7 Just place a short stalk of the pipe cleaner in the top for a stem—and set the pumpkin face out to either cause fright . . . or delight!

HOLIDAY HINTS

Fold your pumpkin form using a 4-inch square (or smaller) piece of paper, and poke a small hole in the bottom. Then use it as a funny pumpkin pencil topper—it makes a great trick-or-treat item!

GOING BATTY

On Halloween night, no one is safe from this blood-crazed creature's bite.

WHAT YOU'LL NEED

- black origami paper
- glue · scissors
- black felt-tip marker · puff paints

DIRECTIONS

1 Begin with a square of black paper in a diamond shape, then fold the bottom point up to meet the top point. Now fold the bottom edge halfway up.

2 Turn the form over, and fold the top point (just the front flap) halfway down. Fold the bottom tip back up ½ inch. You've just made the body and wings of your bat.

3 Take the left side and fold it in half, aligning with the right side. Use a Valley Fold to fold the front flap on the right to the left, then use a Mountain Fold to fold the back flap. These folded flaps are the bat's wings, and they should lay flat against each other.

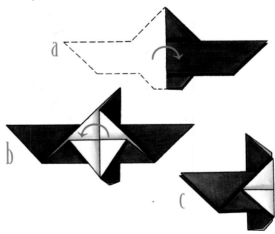

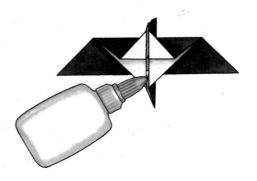

4 Open the wings, so they are spread apart. Glue the area at the back where the wings meet.

5 To make the bat's head, squash-fold Point D by holding the tip and pushing it down flat until it forms a square. Dab some glue inside the head so it lies closer to the body.

6 Using scissors, cut away areas shown by the dotted lines in the illustration. This will form your bat's ears and give a wavy edge to its wings.

7 Secure the head with a dab of glue in the opening, right below the ears. Color any exposed white areas with the black felt-tip marker. Use dots of puff paint to create yellow eyes and a red mouth.

HOLiDAY HiNTS

To make a *real* "bat mobile," glue a crescent-shaped moon cut from cardboard onto a wire hanger, then tie on several origami bats with varying lengths of clear fishing line. Show off your mobile by hanging it in a window or doorway.

HOME, HAUNTED HOME

With its creaky shutters and ghostly apparitions, this haunted house will make your teeth chatter and your knees knock in fright!

WHAT YOU'LL NEED
- origami paper • scissors • glue
- ribbon • black fine-tip marker

DIRECTIONS

1 Begin with Basic Form 3, then fold the right and left bottom corners (top layer only) up to the center point. Turn the form over and repeat this step with the remaining layer.

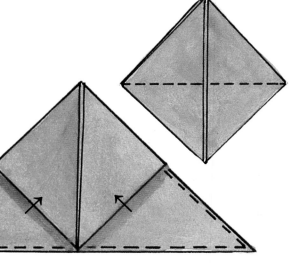

2 You now have a diamond shape. Fold the bottom point up to the top point to make a crease and unfold. Then lift up the triangle on the right side and push on point A to form a square.

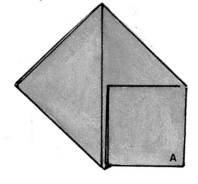

3 Lift up the triangle on the left side and push on point B to form a square.

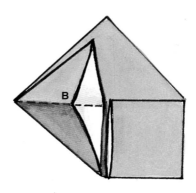

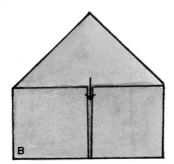

4 Then turn the form over and repeat steps 2 and 3 on the other side.

5 Fold the two outer sides (top layer only) to the center to make a crease, then unfold again. Fold and unfold triangle shapes on each "door," making creases as shown.

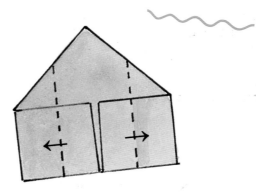

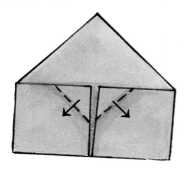

6 To create the large front door, use the creases that you have just made as guidelines and fold point C to meet point A, and point D to meet point B.

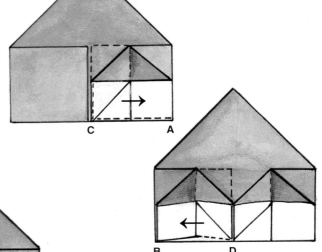

C   A

B   D

7 To finish the form, fold up the center triangle.

8 Now you're ready to decorate! You can follow the picture below as a guide or create your own original house of horrors. Use ribbon, cotton pieces, and whatever else you can find to make this the creep-iest haunt on the block!

THANKSGIVING TURKEY BASKET

This origami turkey is almost life-size to serve as a colorful centerpiece or basket for any holiday table.

WHAT YOU'LL NEED

- large sheet of brown construction paper (about 16 inches square) or a grocery bag, cut into a square
- glue • orange and red puff paints
- feathers • clear tape
- three small red water balloons, not inflated

DIRECTIONS

1. Fold the brown paper into Basic Form 2. Put the form in a diagonal shape, then unfold the upper and lower corners on the right side.

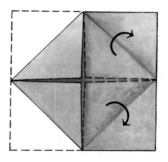

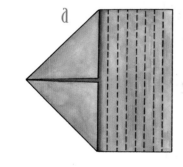

a

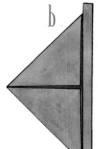

b

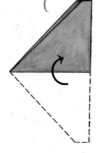

c

2. Next, fold the right side to the center line, using an Accordion Fold. Just take a small strip and fold it over and under several times as though it were a fan. It's okay if this folded strip overlaps the center line a bit. Now use a Mountain Fold to fold the entire form in half.

3 Arrange your shape in front of you so that the fanned-out Accordion Fold is in the upper right section. Fold that section down to the bottom line of the craft. Unfold. Take the lower right corner and make a small crease, ½ inch or so, then unfold. Create a base for your turkey to sit on by making an Inside-Reverse Fold with that right corner. To do this, take Point A, and slightly lift the flap and open it up. Then use your finger to poke the point so it rests inside the form.

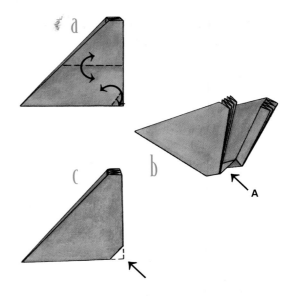

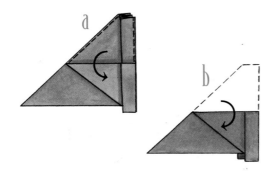

4 Now fold down the tip, using a Valley Fold to fold down the front "wing," and a Mountain Fold to fold down the back.

5 Crease your form again at the areas shown in the illustration. Be sure to make your folds sharp and the next steps will be easy.

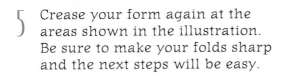

6 First, lift the point at the left side, then use an Inside-Reverse Fold to push it in so that it bends along the farthest crease and stands up straight as you see here. That's the turkey's neck and head.

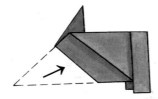

7 See the crease near the tip? Make a beak for your feathered friend by using an Inside-Reverse Fold to fold the tip down so it bends at the crease.

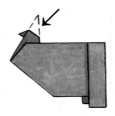

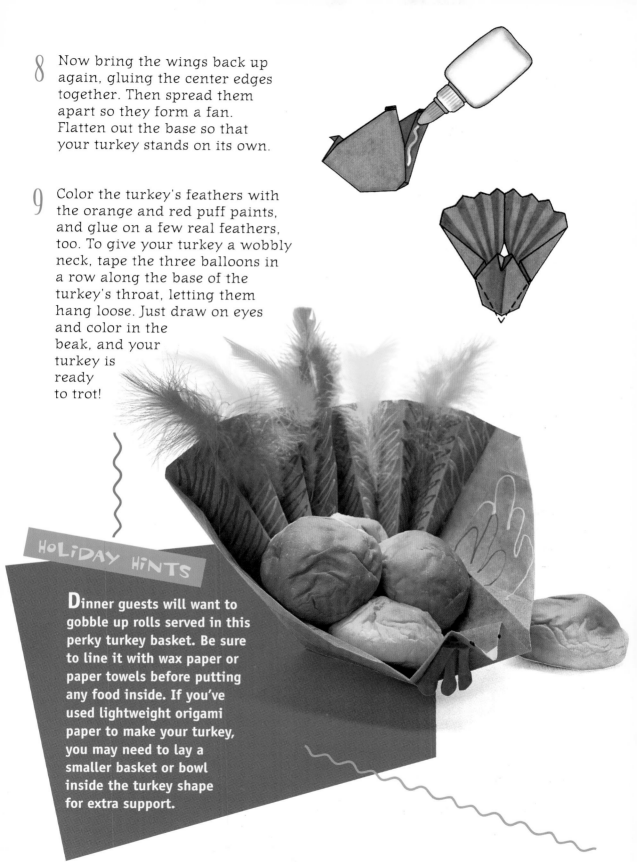

8 Now bring the wings back up again, gluing the center edges together. Then spread them apart so they form a fan. Flatten out the base so that your turkey stands on its own.

9 Color the turkey's feathers with the orange and red puff paints, and glue on a few real feathers, too. To give your turkey a wobbly neck, tape the three balloons in a row along the base of the turkey's throat, letting them hang loose. Just draw on eyes and color in the beak, and your turkey is ready to trot!

HOLIDAY HINTS

Dinner guests will want to gobble up rolls served in this perky turkey basket. Be sure to line it with wax paper or paper towels before putting any food inside. If you've used lightweight origami paper to make your turkey, you may need to lay a smaller basket or bowl inside the turkey shape for extra support.

ROCK-A-BYE PAPOOSE

This little papoose comes wrapped in its own Indian blanket.

WHAT YOU'LL NEED

- origami paper
- brown and pink colored pencils
- fine-tipped black marker
- black yarn • glue
- assorted tiny glass beads
- thread • tape • scissors

DIRECTIONS

1 Begin with a square piece of paper in a flat diamond shape. Bring the right point to meet the left point and crease. Unfold. Now fold the lower left and right sides to the center crease, so your paper looks like a kite. Use a Mountain Fold to fold back the top triangle.

2 Next, fold the top left and right sides in to the center crease and turn your form over.

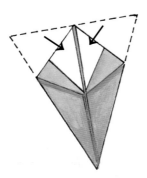

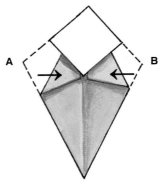

A   B

3 This part is a little tricky, so go slowly. Lift the upper square (the papoose's head), reach inside, and fold points A and B to the center.

4 To complete your papoose form, fold back the top and bottom points on the head, and the bottommost point of the form.

38

5 Using the brown pencil, lightly color in the face. Use the pink pencil to add color to the cheeks. Add features (eyes, nose, and mouth) with the black marker. To get a "baby" look, be sure to draw the features low on the head, leaving the forehead large.

6 Cut a few strands of black yarn for hair. (Remember, babies do not have much hair!) Glue the hair on and allow to dry.

7 Make an Indian necklace for your papoose by stringing some tiny glass beads onto thread. Stop when your string of beads is long enough to go across the front of the baby under the chin. Put the necklace on the papoose and tie the thread with a knot at the back. To keep the necklace from shifting, put a piece of tape on the back, trapping the thread underneath. A spot of glue at the center front will also keep the necklace in place.

8 Decorate the front of the form— the blanket—with cutout zigzags and strips of colorful origami paper. Glue these shapes onto the blanket. Finally, cut out a headband and feather from origami paper and secure them onto the head with glue.

HOLiDAY HiNTS

This little papoose would be a wonderful addition to Mom's Thanksgiving centerpiece. Just glue a Popsicle® stick to the back of the form and place it among the flowers!

CLASSIC HOLIDAY CANDLE

WHAT YOU'LL NEED

- origami paper (red for Christmas or blue for Hanukkah)
- yellow marker
- puff paints, especially gold or silver

The paper flame from this classic-looking candle will brighten up any winter holiday windowsill or tabletop.

DIRECTIONS

1 Begin with your paper in a diamond shape, color side face down. Fold it in half by bringing the left point to the right point, and in half again, bringing the bottom point to the top point. Crease the edges sharply, then unfold the form completely.

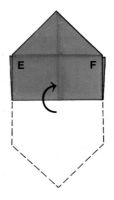

2 Now fold the left, right, and top points to the center line.

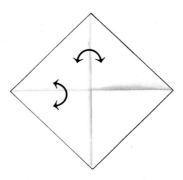

3 Grasp the bottom point and fold it up, so the base of this fold is along the center line.

4 Use a Valley Fold to fold Point E, forming a straight diagonal line from the tip to the bottom of the form. Repeat this step on Point F.

5 Now fold the lower left and right portions to the center line, then slightly reopen.

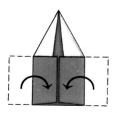

6 Look closely at the inside of the right side. Do you see the diagonal "pockets" at the top and bottom? To round out your candle, you need to insert the left side into the pockets in the right side, sliding the left side in until it holds snugly by itself.

7 Take hold of the flame, about 2 inches below the tip, and twist it around until it forms a small flame shape.

8 Use a yellow marker to add fire to the flame, and with puff paints, draw a festive design on the candle. Now you have a holiday display that's really hot!

HOLIDAY HINTS

A small paper plate makes a great base for your holiday candle. Just tape the candle to the top of the plate and circle it with a sprig of holly or several strands of curled ribbon.

3-D CHRISTMAS TREE

Make a miniature version of a fabulous fir that you can really decorate with garland, candy canes, and even tiny paper chains!

DIRECTIONS

1   Begin with one piece of paper flat in a diamond shape, color side face down, then fold the bottom point up halfway.

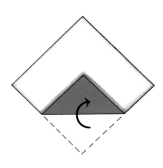

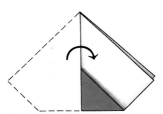

2   Use a Mountain Fold to fold the form in half so that most of the colored side of your paper is on the inside. Turn your form so that the bottom left corner is colored.

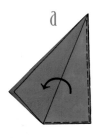

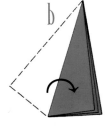

3   Fold the far right corner of the front flap over to the center line and make a sharp crease. Turn the form over and repeat on the other side. Then take the new left edge and again fold into the center line. Turn the tree over, and repeat.

4   Partially pull apart your form, and set it aside. Now repeat Steps 1 through 3 with another sheet of paper to make the other half of your tree.

5 Run a thin line of glue down the two outside edges of one tree half, and attach the other section of the tree to it.

6 Get into the spirit of the season and trim your tree by gluing on all sorts of ornaments like beads, cute magazine cut-outs, ribbon, or even brightly painted uncooked pasta.

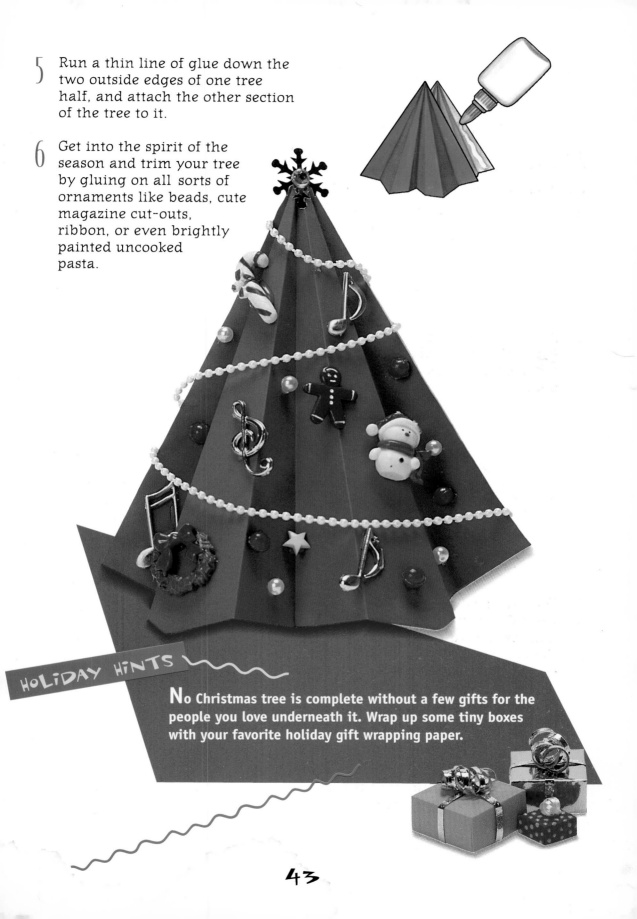

HOLiDAY HiNTS

No Christmas tree is complete without a few gifts for the people you love underneath it. Wrap up some tiny boxes with your favorite holiday gift wrapping paper.

LITTLE HANUKKAH DREIDEL

WHAT YOU'LL NEED

- blue origami paper
- yellow paper • blue pipe cleaner
- scissors • glue

This four-sided, spinning, traditional Hanukkah toy makes a perfect gift.

DIRECTIONS

1 Using the blue paper, begin with Basic Form 3 and fold the left and right bottom corners (front flaps only) to the center. Turn the form over and repeat this step.

a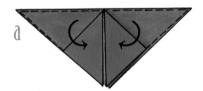

b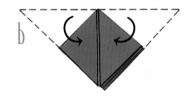

a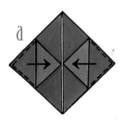

b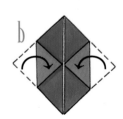

2 Now take the left and right corners (front flaps only) and fold them in to the center line. Turn the form over again and repeat this step on the other side.

3 Take the bottom left and right points (front flaps only) that meet in the center and fold and unfold them to make a sharp crease.

4 Next, take these points and tuck them into the center triangles. To do this, open the triangle pockets with your fingers and slip the edge in. Then turn your form over and repeat Step 3 and this step on the other side.

5 Find the tiny hole at the top of your form. When you blow into it, your dreidel will instantly go from flat to fat.

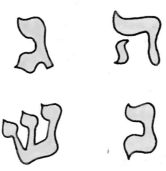

6 To get your dreidel into tip "top" shape, squeeze the form gently and the bottom half will naturally form into a point. Make a sharp crease along each side to the bottom point by pinching the paper.

7 Tuck a 1-inch-long stick of pipe cleaner into the hole as a lid. Put the traditional symbols on the dreidel by tracing the figures shown here onto the yellow paper. Cut them out and paste one on each side.

HOLIDAY HINTS

Children traditionally spin the dreidel, each "betting" a chocolate coin. If a person's top lands on

win the pot of candy

break even

all coins are lost!

45

ANGELIC ORIGAMI

How can paper be angelic? You'll see when you fold this lovely origami angel, which can stand in a window or on a mantel as a perfect holiday decoration.

WHAT YOU'LL NEED

- colored origami paper • flesh-colored origami paper
- fine-line black marker
- pink marker, crayon, or pencil • glue
- pipe cleaners • tape • wire cutters
- scissors • ribbon • doily • glitter paint
- cotton balls

DIRECTIONS

1 Begin with Basic Form 5, with the opening in the back and the two loose triangles pointing down. Then fold the upper left and right sides to the center line.

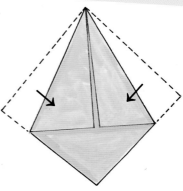

2 Next, unfold the back flaps. These will soon be the angel's wings.

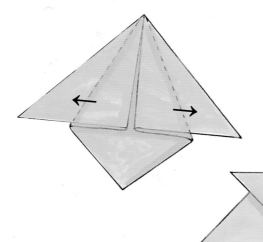

3 Now fold point A over to the left and crease it well; then fold it back to the right as shown.

a

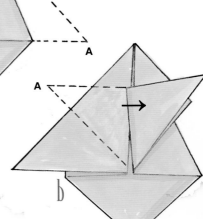

b

46

4 You now have a little flap across the center line. This is point B. Use a Valley Fold to fold it in the same direction as point A.

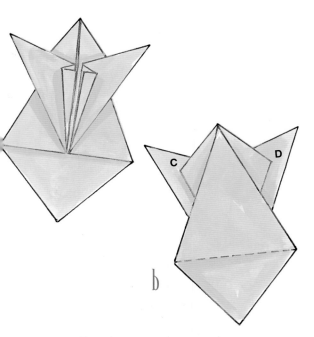

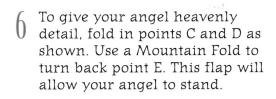

b

5 Repeat steps 3 and 4 on the left side of the form, then turn the form over.

6 To give your angel heavenly detail, fold in points C and D as shown. Use a Mountain Fold to turn back point E. This flap will allow your angel to stand.

7 Now it's time to add the details. For the head, cut out two circles of the same size from the flesh-colored origami paper. On one of the circles, draw a sweet face using the fine-line black marker. Color in cheeks using a pink marker, crayon, or pencil.

8 Attach the head by spreading glue onto the white sides of both circles. Take the angel body, front side up, and place it on top of the glued side of the blank circle. Make sure to overlap the body at least ½ inch as shown. Now carefully place the circle with the face on top of the body, making sure to align it with the other circle. The result should be that the body is "sandwiched" between both circles.

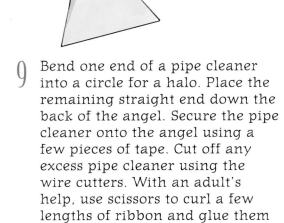

9 Bend one end of a pipe cleaner into a circle for a halo. Place the remaining straight end down the back of the angel. Secure the pipe cleaner onto the angel using a few pieces of tape. Cut off any excess pipe cleaner using the wire cutters. With an adult's help, use scissors to curl a few lengths of ribbon and glue them on for hair.

10 For the final touches, cut a small piece of paper doily for a lace collar and glue it on under the chin. Add sparkle to the wings with glitter paint. Place a fluffy cloud of cotton balls around the base of your angel.

HOLIDAY HINTS

Create an angel tree by making several angels and hanging them on the tree as holiday ornaments. Tie a loop of thread onto the halo for hanging. At the very top of the tree, why not make a large golden halo with yellow pipe cleaners—how angelic!